Major League SOCCER

Montreal Impact

John Bankston

Mitchell Lane
PUBLISHERS

Printing   1   2   3   4   5   6   7   8

First Edition, 2020.
Author: John Bankston
Designer: Ed Morgan
Editor: Lisa Petrillo

Series: Major League Soccer
Title: Montreal Impact / by John Bankston

Hallandale, FL : Mitchell Lane Publishers, [2020]

Library bound ISBN: 9781680204803
eBook ISBN: 9781680204810

Contents

Words in **bold** throughout
can be found in the Glossary.

Montreal Gets Its Shot

CHAPTER ONE

Major League Soccer (MLS) was expanding north of the U.S.-Canada border. For more than ten years, the only MLS teams were in the United States. Beginning in 2007, the League went to Canada. Montreal was ready.

Montreal is second largest city in Canada, and part of Quebec. The French-speaking province is three times bigger than Texas. Despite the cold winter weather, the city loves soccer.

The city's Olympic **Stadium** provides a roof for soccer and baseball teams. It took almost ten years to build the roof. Designed for the 1976 Olympics, the stadium was part of many new sporting facilities that cost Quebec more than one billion dollars. The summer heat didn't stop more than 70,000 soccer fans from pouring into the new stadium. Team Captain Jimmy Douglas scored Canada's only goals in losing men's soccer matches against the North Korean and Soviet Union teams.

Ten years later, the men's team reached the finals of the World Cup. The Cup is soccer's most important **tournament**. Every four years, 32 teams compete. Many more teams don't **qualify**. The 1986 World Cup was the only time Canada qualified.

The U.S. dream of hosting the World Cup is why Major League Soccer began. In order to host, the country first needed a top-tier pro team. Leagues like the American **Professional** Soccer League (APSL) and the National Soccer League had teams in both the U.S. and Canada. To get the World Cup, the U.S. had to create a league with just U.S. teams.

Major League sports attract the best players in the world. They are paid the most money. Their teams have the strongest fan support. In 1996, soccer got its own Major League. In 1994, the U.S. hosted the World Cup. Two years later, MLS began.

Soccer is played by more than 250 million people. It is the world's most popular game.

The game reached Canada in the 1800s. It was brought over by **immigrants**. People who played in England and France also played in their new home. In 1904, Canada sent its men's soccer team to the Olympics for the first time. The team won the Gold Medal.

At first, professional soccer struggled in Montreal. The Montreal Manic only lasted from 1981 to 1983. The Impact had a bigger impact. The team joined APSL in 1993. Owner Joey Saputo believed the city's soccer fans were ready to support a top-level team. The Impact players proved they could compete. Before the season ended, they enjoyed a seven-game winning streak. They still finished dead last.

The team improved. The Impact reached the playoffs five years in a row. They were often atop the standings. They won playoffs against teams like the Staten Island Vipers and the Los Angeles Salsa, where Goalkeeper Pat Harrington played with such determination he blocked the goal with his face.

The second year was one of the Impact's best. In Montreal, the Claude Robillard Stadium was sold out. The team faced the reigning champs, the Colorado Foxes. Despite their title, the Foxes were outfoxed. They couldn't score. The Impact got the game's only goal—thanks to a successful free kick by Jean Harbor. Thousands of overjoyed soccer fans ran onto the field. They had a lot to celebrate for the city's first North American soccer title. In 2004, Impact players did it again—beating the Rochester Raging Rhinos.

In 2009, Montreal won the 2009 USL First Division title. Two years later, the team joined the North American Soccer League. By then MLS had changed the rules. The League would expand to Canada.

In 2012, the Montreal Impact played its first MLS season. Today there are 20 teams in the U.S., with three from Canada. In 2019, Cincinnati, Ohio will get its first MLS team. The next year, new teams will come to Miami, Florida and Nashville, Tennessee.

Justin Braun (*left*) of the Montreal Impact chest bumps the ball as Chicago Fire's Logan Pause moves in on March 17, 2012.

In MLS, teams compete in two divisions. Montreal is in the Eastern Conference, along with Toronto FC. The Vancouver Whitecaps are in the Western Conference. During the regular season, every team plays 17 games at home and 17 away. The regular season runs March–October.

Teams earn three points for every win. Tie scores give each team one point. Losses earn zero points. In October, the top 12 teams by points enter the playoffs with half from each Conference. The final two teams compete in the MLS Championship during December.

By 2015, the average MLS game attracted more than 21,000 fans. The League was more popular than ones in France or Brazil. That year, Montreal Impact players showed off their skills to the rest of North America.

Fun Facts

1 The 2026 World Cup will be played in North America. Matches will be played in the U.S., Mexico and Canada—including Montreal.

2 Because host countries get into the tournament automatically, Canada will have a team in the World Cup. It will be the first one in forty years.

3 In 2018, of the 637 MLS players, 315—almost half—were born in a country other than the U.S. or Canada.

The Impact Finds Its Footing

CHAPTER TWO

Andreas Romero slipped the two defenders. The game was almost over. He stood more than 30 feet from the goal. He kicked. He scored.

Romero made the winning goal and helped make history. Montreal Impact had just beaten Costa Rica's Alajuelense in two games. For the first time, a Canadian team would play in the CONCACAF Champion League's finals.

The Confederation of North, Central American and Caribbean Association Football (CONCACAF) championship brings together the region's top teams. It is North America's most important **international** tournament. The winning team qualifies for the World Cup.

"We are very happy with what we've been able to accomplish and now our goal is to win the Cup," Impact defender Bakary Soumare told a reporter from Canada's *The Globe and Mail* in 2015. Even die-hard fans doubted the team would reach the finals. In the last 46 regular season matches, the Impact had only won seven times.

Competing in the CONCACAF, the U.S. and Canada usually field MLS teams. The winning team is almost always from Mexico. That country's teams have won 34 titles.

On April 29, 2015, Impact fans imagined a different ending. The Finals were held at Montreal's Olympic Stadium. More than 61,000 spectators watched as the Impact's Andres Romero scored the first goal. At halftime, Mexican team Club América was down a goal.

They came back in the second half. Club América won 5–3 over the Impact. Despite the loss, it showed that Montreal players could compete against some of the best in the world.

Andres Romero (15) scores a goal against Club América during the first half of the game on April 29, 2015.

The Montreal Impact began playing in 2012. The League believed strong fan support for the USL team would continue. Plus, the owner already had the right kind of stadium.

When MLS began, the ten teams usually shared stadiums. Soccer fields were also used for football or baseball.

The field where a team plays is called the pitch. New York City FC's first season was in 2015. Despite being a new team, New York plays in Yankee Stadium, sharing the field with the city's baseball team. It's too narrow for soccer. It's hard to see the game from many seats in the stands. It's often ranked the worst home pitch in MLS.

Sharing a pitch with a football team isn't much better. The New England Revolution share Gillette Stadium with the National Football League's New England Patriots. The stadium seats more than 66,000. Since the Revolution's home games attract less than 20,000 fans, it looks empty.

Although Century Link Field was designed for NFL's Seattle Seahawks, the Sounders are so popular that fans almost fill the huge stadium. More than 43,000 regularly show up.

Like the Impact, Stade Saputo was built before the team entered the League. The team and the stadium were designed to grow.

Montreal Impact play
Columbus Crew at Saputo
Stadium in July 2012.

On May 19, 2008, the Impact played its first home game at Stade
Saputo. The match against Vancouver ended in a scoreless draw.
The new stadium cost more than $17 million and held 13,000 fans.
Built just for soccer, it was constructed atop a running track in
Olympic Park.

In 2011, stadium **expansion** began. The Québec government
contributed more than $23 million, with seating expanded to
20,000. Because players complain that they can get injured on
artificial turf, the field would use natural grass.

In 2012, the Impact's first season started badly. The team played in Vancouver and lost the March 10th game to the Whitecaps 2–0. Because the new stadium wasn't finished, the Impact's first home game was played in Olympic Stadium. More than 58,000 showed up and broke a thirty-year record for pro soccer attendance. Montreal tied the Chicago Fire with one goal each.

Next the team endured a three-game losing streak in away games. Fans and players remained hopeful for the most important game still to come. Montreal was playing its **rival**, Toronto FC.

More than 23,000 people watched as the Montreal-Toronto game cruised toward a tie. With just nine minutes left in the game, Andrew Wenger scored. The forward had been the Impact's number one draft pick. Now he helped his team win its first home game with a 2–1 victory.

Just a few months later, fans enjoyed another win in their redesigned stadium. On June 12, just over 17,000 watched as the Impact beat the Seattle Sounders 4–1 in Stade Saputo. Unfortunately the season had too few moments like that one. The team lost 16 games the first season.

In 2013, the Impact won the Canadian Championship, beating both Vancouver and Toronto. The next year, Montreal would win again.

In 2013, the Impact team-members had another reason to celebrate when they had reached the playoffs. Then in 2014, the Impact lost 18 games, becoming the lowest-ranked team in the MLS.

The next year, Montreal reached the playoffs. Impact players won in the knockout round against a scoreless Toronto and reached the semi finals. In 2016, they made it all the way to the Finals. With two matches, the combined score put Toronto ahead 7–5.

The 2017 season was a disappointment with only 11 wins and 17 losses. Still fan support remained strong and attendance high.

After Head Coach Mauro Biello was fired in 2017, Rémi Garde became the team's fifth coach in six seasons. He changed the team's style. He did this by focusing on the attack.

Fun Facts

1 The team's colors for home games are blue and black. On away games, players wear blue and white.

2 The Montreal Impact logo includes a shield of silver, black, blue, and white with four silver stars. It also has the team's motto: *Tous Pour Gagner* (French for *All For Victory*).

The Way Montreal Plays

I t's not easy taking your game on the road. Soccer players get used to their home pitch. They know the field. They know the conditions. Best of all they have fans, the cheering crowd teams call the "12th player."

Traveling means flying, staying in hotels, time zone changes, and eating out.

Facing a pair of away games on the thousands of miles across Canada, Coach Rémi Garde told *The Montreal Gazette* in July 2018 that, "I will try to be attentive to everything: nutrition, diet, recovery. In France, we call that invisible preparation."

In Portland, the Impact faced a team with some of the strongest fan support in the League. The Timbers had sold-out more than 100 home games in a row. The team was enjoying a 12-game winning streak. And the players hadn't lost all season at their home pitch.

Coach Remi Garde

The Impact had a 9–12 record. Yet Impact players realized the road trip would help them as a team. Players grow closer when they don't go home at night. "It will be a good experience for the group," fullback Daniel Lovitz told the *Gazette*. "It's an exciting time for us."

Part of the excitement came from having a new coach. When Garde was hired the Impact had reached the playoffs three times. They also had three losing seasons. The coach felt a more aggressive, attacking style of play would help the team live up to its name. The best way to make an impact was to keep possession of the ball and take it to the opponent's goal. In the July 21st game against the Timbers, even the coach got aggressive.

Going into halftime, the Impact led the Timbers 2–1. Could Montreal break Portland's streak?

The Timber's only goal had come during the first half when Goalkeeper Evan Bush dropped a high ball. Samuel Armenteros kicked the ball into the net for the Timber's score.

Chapter Three

In the 65th minute of play, the Timber's Diego Valeri used his head. Coach Garde believed he also used his hands. The Timber's Sebastian Blanco had raced toward the goal and driven the ball toward the net. Bush smacked it into the air with both hands. Valeri leaped up and nailed a header for the score.

Garde was certain Valeri had used his hands. If he had, the goal would not have counted. When the goal was allowed, Garde argued so loudly he was kicked out of the game.

The tie gave the Timbers a 13-game streak. The Impact had started the season winning just three games and losing ten. Yet by the time they reached Portland, the Montreal players had improved. In their last eight games, they enjoyed a 6–2 record.

The improvement in the Impact's play and the issues about the use of hands are why understanding the basics are so important. Soccer can be easy to learn. Yet even pros have a hard time mastering it.

Eleven players line up on each side. Goalkeepers like Evan Bush are the only players allowed to use their hands. Other players can only use their feet and their head.

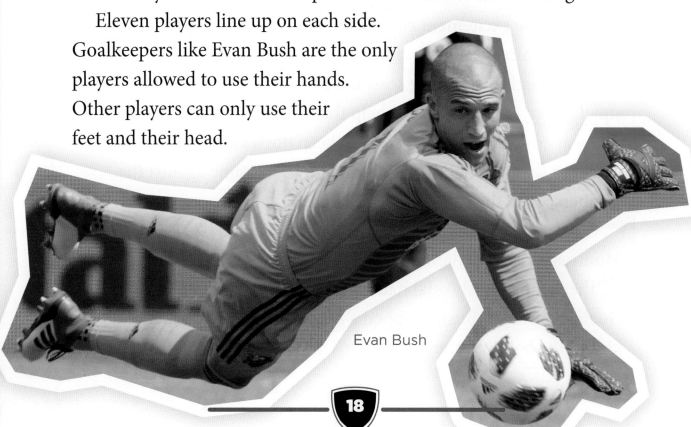

Evan Bush

Players usually use a 4-4-2 formation. The two forwards remain close to their opponent's goal, focused on sending the ball into the goal.

In the middle of the field are four midfielders. Defending midfielders try to keep the ball out of their team's goal. Attacking midfielders drive the ball toward the other team's goal. Keeping the ball in play like a midfielder is a hard job. The team leader or captain is often the center midfielder.

Soccer has two halves, 45 minutes each. The clock doesn't stop during pauses in play.

Although every game is the same length, Impact fans sometimes felt like games against Toronto FC last longer. The two cities had been rivals long before the MLS existed.

Quebec was once the largest province in Canada. Today, Quebec is home to just more than eight million people. Toronto's home province of Ontario has 13.4 million.

"I've played in some big rivalries," Toronto defender Drew Moor told *The Globe and Mail* in 2017. "But there's something different about this one. It's not just a rivalry in sports, it's a rivalry in language. It's almost an eerie feeling when I'm walking on the streets of Montreal and I pass some Impact fans."

Fun Fact

The team mascot is Tac-Tik, a happy, slightly chubby dog.

Montreal Impact's Top Players

CHAPTER FOUR

Over their seven seasons of play, Montreal Impact players are among the highest ranked in the League. Here are a few:

Marco Di Vaio
Striker (2012–2014)

With 34 goals in 76 appearances, Di Vaio was a big reason the Impact players reached the playoffs their second year. He also helped them win the Canadian Championships in 2013 and 2014. Born in Rome, Italy, he was voted the team's Most Valuable Player in 2013 and was the top scorer in both 2013 and 2014.

Patrice Bernie
Midfielder (2012–2017)

Joining the team in its first year, no other Impact player has had as many appearances as this Canadian. Playing in 151 matches for the MLS Impact, he also appeared 73 times in 2000–2002 when the team was in the USL. As Captain, he helped the Impact reach the finals of the CONCACAF Champions League in 2015. The next year, he guided the team to the playoffs. He retired at the end of the 2017 season at age 38.

Hassoun Camara
Defender; Full Back (2012–2017)

French-born Camara began his Impact career when it was in the NASL in 2011. After being named the Impact's Most Valuable Player, he was signed to the team when it joined the MLS team. During his second season, he scored the game winning goal in the Canadian Championship. The victory qualified the team for the CONCACAF Champions League. He retired in 2017 due to injuries.

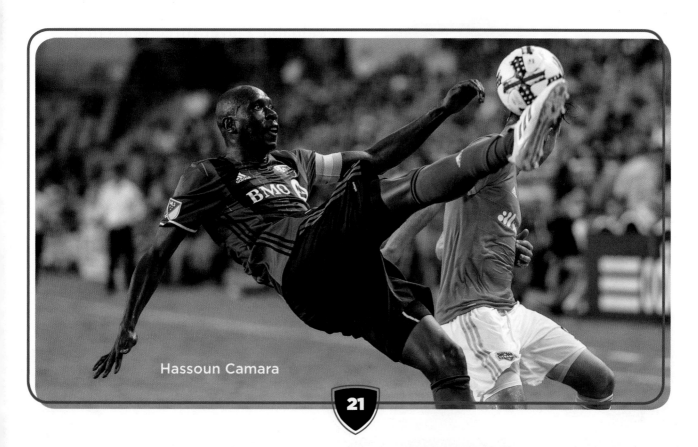

Hassoun Camara

Evan Bush
Goalkeeper (2012–present)

With more than 130 appearances, Ohio native Bush has covered the net for the Impact since the team's early days in the MLS. Although he only made 15 appearances in three seasons, from 2015 on he has been the team's regular goalkeeper. In 2015, he was nominated for the 2015 CONCACAF Goalkeeper of the Year award and won the Champions League Golden Glove award.

Ignacio Piatti
Midfielder (2014–current)

Number 10 on the field but No. 1 in goals scored for both 2016 and 2017, Argentinian Piatti has had a huge impact on the Impact. In over 100 appearances, Piatti has scored over 60 goals. Besides being the team's top scorer in 2016 and 2017, he was voted the Montreal Impact Most Valuable Player three years in a row from 2015 to 2017. He has also appeared three times in the MLS All-Star Game.

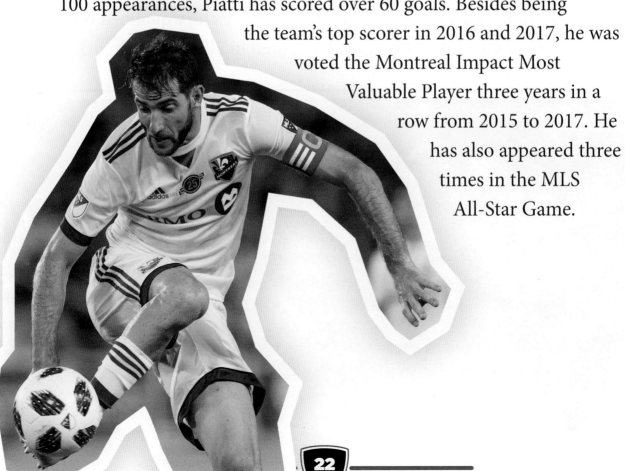

Didier Drogba
Striker (2015-2016)

The high-scoring Drogba was born in Africa's Ivory Coast. During the first season, he averaged a goal a game for the first 11 games. In 2015, he helped the Impact reach the playoffs and defeat rival Toronto FC 3–0. Although he did not play as well in his second season, he did score his team's only goal in the 2016 MLS All-Star where MLS lost to Britain's the Arsenal.

Didier Drogba (*bottom*) challenges LA Galaxy defender Daniel Steres for the ball in May 2016.

Fun Facts

1 A five-foot-tall bell called the North Star is rung after the Impact scores a goal or wins a game.

2 Fan group Ultras Montreal travels to matches against the Philadelphia Union, New England Revolution, D.C. United, New York Red Bulls, and main rival Toronto FC.

Montreal Communicates

There are a lot of languages spoken in the Impact locker room. There are players who speak English. Others speak mainly Spanish or Italian. To get around Montreal, it helps to know a little French. New players struggle. That's why **veterans** help them out. They believe being a team is about more than what you do on the field. What you do off of it matters as well.

"I try to help a little with translating," Defensive midfielder Samuel Piette told a reporter for *The Montreal Gazette* in February 2018. He speaks French along with English and Spanish. "Take someone like Jeisson [Andrés Vargas Salazar] for example, who does not speak English and only Spanish. [The other players] can help him a little." The forward had signed with the team just the month before. Already others were helping the native of the South American country of Chile.

Every team can have up to eight international players. MLS teams once used older European stars. Now many come from South America. Even in far away Montreal, there are a number of players like Salazar. Besides Chile, players like Victor Cabrera and Ignacio Piatti hail from Argentina. Alejandro Silva is from Uruguay.

"There are thousands and thousands of talented [players] in South America that are just waiting for an opportunity," Vancouver Whitecaps head coach Carl Robinson told *Sports Illustrated* in 2018. "These players want to be coached. They love football. And I want to work with players like that, because they know the game."

For Coach Rémi Garde, finding the best players was sometimes a challenge. As he admitted to Sportsnet.ca newssite, "If you look at all the players that came in since I'm here, I'm not sure if one or two have changed the game. You cannot always change the game."

Chapter Five

In Montreal the game was the same. It just came with a French accent. Joining the Impact meant playing *le football*. A header was a *frappe de la tête*. The goalkeeper was also called the *gardien de but*. *Un but* was a goal.

When the Impact began, it might have been less noticed than other teams. Across the MLS, there are many Spanish-speaking players. They are usually translated for English audiences. Plus, Major League Soccer has millions of Spanish-speaking fans. In Montreal, Spanish-speaking players focused on learning French. Outside of Quebec, the team didn't have strong fan support.

Coach Garde admits he is sometimes challenged by the English language. He blames his ejection from a game against the Timbers on that misunderstanding. Yet the blend of cultures and languages is part of what makes Major League Soccer special. No other pro sports league has players from as many different places in the world. The Impact coaches are from France. Many of their players are from other countries. Italian center Matteo Mancosu doesn't think that matters. "We understand the language of soccer," he told *The Montreal Gazette* in February of 2018. "There's a few ways we can converse: in English, and even French is similar to Italian. We can understand each other in many ways."

For the Impact and its fans, it's about more than just understanding. It's about love. In a season where very few MLS teams have winning records, the Impact's new coach, aggressive players and love of the game may help it reach the playoffs.

Fun Fact

In 2018, the Montreal Impact had players from Algeria, Argentina, Belize, Finland, France, Italy, Japan, Uruguay, and Italy. They also had nine players born in Quebec.

What You Should Know

- Soccer is the world's most popular game. Almost 250 million people play the sport.

- A soccer-like game was used to train Chinese soldiers 2,000 years ago.

- Greeks and Romans also played a sport like soccer.

- The game as it is now played probably started in England some 1800 years ago. It celebrated a victory in battle over invaders from Rome.

- In 1314, British King Edward II made playing soccer illegal.

- The name soccer came from England.

- The United States, Canada, Japan, Korea, and Southeast Asia are among the few places that do not call the game football.

- In 2018, of the 637 MLS players, 315—almost half—were born in a country other than the U.S. or Canada. The top five by country are Argentina with 23, England and France with 19, Ghana with 18 and Columbia with 15.

- The team has reached the MLS playoffs three times.

- The Impact has had three seasons with more losses than wins.

Quick Stats

2013, 2014	Wins Canadian Championships
2013, 2015, 2016	Reaches MLS Playoffs

1642 Montreal, the largest city in the Canadian province of Quebec is founded.

1877 Montreal's Dominion Football Association begins competing, playing mainly college teams from the province of Ontario.

1904 The Canadian men's soccer team wins a gold medal at the Olympic Games in St. Louis, Missouri.

1925 Montreal hosts Canada's first home Men's International Friendly match against the U.S.

1976 Montreal hosts the Olympics and the men's national soccer team reaches the finals.

1983 Professional soccer team the Montreal Manic (Manic de Montréal) plays in the North American Soccer League.

1985 The Canadian team wins the CONCACAF Championship for the first time. The tournament runs between 1963 and 1989.

1986 Canada's men's team reaches the World Cup finals for the first and last time.

1993 Montreal Impact begins play in the American Professional Soccer League (APSL).

1994 Montreal Impact wins the APSL championship.

2000 Entering the CONCACAF Gold Cup ranked 85th in the world, Canada wins the final, defeating Colombia 2–0.

2004 The team wins its second APSL championship.

2008 Now part of the United Soccer League's First Division, the Impact begins playing in a new soccer-specific stadium, Stade Saputo.

2009 The Impact wins a third championship (in a non-MLS league).

2012 The Impact plays its first game at the now-expanded Stade Saputo, beating the Seattle Sounders FC 4–1.

2015 Montreal Impact becomes the first Canadian team to reach the finals of the CONCACAF Champion League.

2018 Built a winning record over the summer.

Glossary

expansion
In sports, an expansion team is one added to a league's original line-up

immigrants
People who move to a country from somewhere else

international
Players who come from other countries

professional
Performing a job for money

qualify
To get accepted into an event or program

rival
Team competing with another for the same goal

stadium
A large arena for sports like soccer

tournament
A competition with contests between many teams until one team is the final winner

veteran
An experienced player

Further Reading

Deborah Crisfield. *The Everything Kids Soccer Book*. Simon and Schuster, 2013.

Deborah Lock. *Soccer School*. DK Publishing, 2015.

Ann Killion. *Champions of Men's Soccer*. Philomel Books, 2018.

Ryan Nagelhout. *Soccer: Who Does What?* Gareth Stevens Publishing, 2018.

Grant Wahl. *Masters of Modern Soccer Crown*, 2018.

Mark Woods. *Goal! Soccer Facts and Stats*. Gareth Stevens, 2011.

On the Internet

Beginners Guide to Soccer, U.S. National Soccer Team Players
https://ussoccerplayers.com/beginners-guide-to-soccer

Montreal Impact Players
https://www.impactMontreal.com/en/players

Soccer Positions
ducksters.com, http://www.ducksters.com/sports/soccer/positions.php

Stade Saputo
https://www.impactMontreal.com/en/stadium/stade-saputo

Index

About the Author

Growing up, I often visited my uncle in Montreal. I really enjoyed writing about the city's devoted soccer fans and its cross-country rivalries. During my time in Portland, Oregon, I knew when the Timbers had a home game. Along the city's West Side, those 17 games created a parade. Fans gathered at restaurants, and crossed the road to the stadium in large groups. Everywhere members of the Timbers Army chanted and cheered. In 2014, the World Cup motivated restaurants to set up tables and giant TV screens in parking lots. Fans arrived sporting the colors of just about every team that qualified. This is what I love about soccer. It's what I love about all sports. For me the most interesting part of a game is how fans and teams relate to one another. The way fans are honored, even celebrated in soccer seems to be unique in sports. The Montreal team draws such devoted fans, and its cross-country rivals made the playing so exciting to see.   —**John Bankston**